MW00570784

Highland Light, North Truro, Cape Cod, Mass. Antique postcard. From Grafton, *Six Old-Time New England Lighthouse Cards*, © 1995 Dover Publications, Inc.

HIGHLAND LIGHT, NORTH TRURO, CAPE COD, MASS.

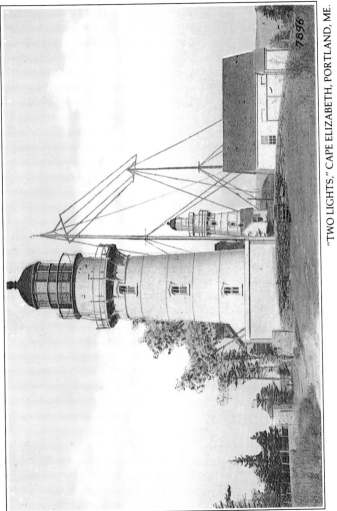

"TWO LIGHTS," CAPE ELIZABETH, PORTLAND, ME.

7896

OLD ORCHARD, WOOD ISLAND LIGHT, ME.

SEGUIN LIGHT, MOUTH OF THE KENNEBEC, ME.

Gay Head Lighthouse, Martha's Vineyard, Mass. Antique postcard. From Grafton, *Six Old-Time New England Lighthouse Cards*, © 1995 Dover Publications, Inc.

GAY HEAD LIGHTHOUSE, MARTHA'S VINEYARD, MASS.

RACE POINT LIGHTHOUSE, PROVINCETOWN, MASS.

Race Point Lighthouse, Provincetown, Mass. Antique postcard. From Grafton, *Six Old-Time New England Lighthouse Cards*, © 1995 Dover Publications, Inc.